MONTPELIER

Images of Vermont's Capital City

PAUL A. CARNAHAN & BILL FISH

THE
History
PRESS

Published by The History Press
Charleston, SC   29403
www.historypress.net

All photos are courtesy of the Vermont Historical Society unless otherwise noted.

First published 2008
Second printing 2011

ISBN 978-1-5402-1890-2

Library of Congress Cataloging-in-Publication Data

Carnahan, Paul A.
Montpelier : images of Vermont's capital city / Paul A. Carnahan and Bill Fish.
p. cm.
ISBN 978-1-5402-1890-2
1. Montpelier (Vt.)--History. 2. Montpelier (Vt.)--History--Pictorial works. I. Fish, Bill. II. Title.
F59.M7 C37
974.3'4--dc22
2008035234

Notice: The information in this book is true and complete to the best of our knowledge. It is offered without guarantee on the part of the authors or The History Press. The authors and The History Press disclaim all liability in connection with the use of this book.

Contents

Introduction

Nestled on the eastern edge of the Green Mountains in the heart of Vermont is Montpelier, the smallest capital city in the country. Colonel Jacob Davis and a group of associates received a charter for the town on August 14, 1781. No one really knows why the name of "Montpelier" was chosen, except that it was probably named after the French city Montpellier. Davis, who had never visited France, but who named the neighboring town Calais, seems to have liked the sound of the towns' names and their association with French politics and culture.

Davis, a Revolutionary War veteran, built a small log cabin here in 1787 and began clearing extremely dense forest land in the area with two of his sons. It wasn't long before he was able to have the rest of his large family join him from the neighboring town of Brookfield. Davis's Montpelier house would soon become a way station for potential settlers scouting the area. Eventually the town founder built yet a bigger house for his family as he helped organize the village, with the aid of incoming settlers. It was a whirlwind of activity for a few years, as the early town leaders scrambled to balance the physically demanding tasks of clearing land and surveying roads with the administrative ones of creating governments and associations.

The growth of infant Montpelier was steady at first, with a population of 113 recorded in 1791 to 890 by 1800. The village, or "hollow," developed around Davis's house near the confluence of the North Branch and Winooski River. Other settlements formed uphill from the village in the Center, East Montpelier and North Montpelier. In 1848, the residents of the village petitioned to separate from the rest of the town, which then became East Montpelier. Montpelier was incorporated as a city in 1894 and annexed a section of Berlin in 1898. By 1860, Montpelier had registered 2,411 inhabitants and had grown to 6,266 by 1900. The city's greatest population was 8,782 people in 1960.

The most prominent factor setting Montpelier apart from other Vermont towns is that in 1805 it was chosen as the state capital. Montpelier was picked over larger towns such as Burlington and Rutland for the permanent home of the legislature because it was not associated with either the eastern or western sides of the state. Additional incentive to choose Montpelier was provided by its inhabitants, who contributed generously to build the first State House. Fortunately for the tax-paying residents, two-thirds of a special State House tax was allowed to be paid in grain, butter or cheese at the going cash price.

Not everyone was impressed by the choice of Montpelier as the capital. Timothy Dwight, the president of Yale University and a respected religious leader, commented,

First known image of Montpelier, by Sarah I. Watrous, 1821. This woodcut was created only thirty-four years after Colonel Jacob Davis first settled here and just thirteen years after the legislature first met in the newly constructed State House in Montpelier. The building to the left of the State House is probably the first courthouse, which was moved to Court Street on the other side of the capitol when the second State House was constructed in 1837. The church building that appears to be located at the north end of Main Street is thought to be the Old Brick Church, the predecessor to Bethany Church, on Main and School Streets.

"A little town, when the seat of government, will always impart its littleness to the legislature and to all its coadjutors." By the 1930s, the appreciation for Montpelier's physical attributes had grown. The WPA guide to Vermont opines, "The choice [of Montpelier as the state capital] was happy in an accidental respect, for this small gap city on the main pass through the Green Mountains is cupped in wooded hills and lines the banks of peaceful streams, thus properly representing the State of valley towns."

The philanthropic assistance of Montpelier's citizens was a large factor in maintaining Montpelier's capital designation. When the state needed a larger, much more permanent structure for a State House only twenty-five years after the initial one was occupied in 1808, the residents didn't blink. This time they collectively donated $15,000 to make it happen.

Images of very early Montpelier are rare. The earliest known drawing of Montpelier was made by Sarah I. Watrous in 1821. Although it is only a rough woodcut, it illustrates the general location of early structures and is the only known image of the town made within its first forty years. The image was updated at least once to show the creation of the second State House (see color insert). Fortunately, the second State House stood long enough to reach the dawn of the photographic era, but just barely. There are only three known photographic images of this imposing structure, which burned to the ground in 1857.

Though illustrations of Montpelier from its beginnings until the advent of photography in the 1840s and 1850s are scarce, the post-1850s record left by early photographers is quite rich. Perhaps due to the political prominence of Montpelier, there were many photographers who took up residence and set up studios in Montpelier, collectively leaving behind a vast legacy of work. Among these early local artists were Frank F. Currier, Charles H. Freeman, Hermon E. Slayton, Seth W. Corse, Alonzo C. Harlow, Azil N. Blanchard, Erwin C. Ayers, Stephen T. Newcomb, Robert Wilkinson and Edwin T. Houston. Their work, along with that of many others, graces the pages of this volume, and we are forever indebted to these prolific documentarians.

Chapter 1

Growth of a Village

Leading a team of surveyors, Jacob Davis first marked the corners of Montpelier in June 1786. Davis, an energetic forty-seven-year-old Revolutionary War veteran, played a vital role in the early growth of Montpelier, as would several of his descendants. Not only is he credited with building the first home in the area (near what would soon become the corner of State and Elm Streets), he is also said to have been tireless when it came to clearing forestland. Driven to make Montpelier attractive to homesteaders, Davis engaged his entire family over a two-year period (1788–89) to clear land in the area from the North Branch to where the Pavilion would eventually be built. They built roads and erected both a sawmill and a gristmill. In 1790, Davis built a bigger home for his family, the first frame house in Montpelier.

Within a few years, many frame houses were constructed as more and more land was cleared. The prominent Cadwell House, built by James Hawkins in the early 1790s, was reputed to be the fifth house constructed in town. Hawkins also was responsible for the first tavern (the first of three versions of the Union House) in 1793. Main Street, and what would be called State Street in 1807 (when the first State House was constructed), were the recipients of most of these early architectural endeavors, as downtown Montpelier began to take shape.

Geographically, downtown Montpelier took advantage of its proximity to the Onion River, eventually called the Winooski (the Abenaki word for "onion"), as well as the North Branch and the Dog River. It was also surrounded by several hills that were covered with thick forests, allowing the logging industry to thrive for many decades, as it did in most of the state. By the late 1800s, in fact, logging had almost completely decimated the forests, and photos of the period bear testimony to the bare landscape.

Thanks mainly to the ease of acquiring material, wooden structures were predominant in downtown Montpelier from the 1790s to the 1870s, and encompassed a fairly diverse range of architectural styles. Of course, with wood came the possibility of fire, and Montpelier was reasonably lucky for a number of decades that its fires were fairly small and innocuous. Town biographer D.P. Thompson was very impressed that he could only count twenty-four fires through 1860. Montpelier, however, would finally learn a hard lesson in 1875, when two major fires devastated the downtown landscape. Suddenly, brick replaced wood as the material of choice, and the look of the busiest downtown streets changed almost overnight. In fact, brick had been used for some of Montpelier's early larger structures (churches, for example), thanks in part to a brickyard that was established just off Main Street in the early 1800s.

Homes were more immune to the city's sudden fear of fire, however, and wooden homes continued to be constructed. Montpelier transitioned through a variety of different architectural styles as it grew slowly. As a result, streets in the city are graced with a variety of architectural styles spanning a range of about two hundred years. Federal, Colonial Revival, French Second Empire, Neoclassical, Italianate, Craftsman, Stick and Shingle are some of the styles that still grace the city's streets.

Often, homes as well as industrial buildings would receive significant face-lifts. Montpelier's first train station, a relatively unattractive "box" completed in 1852, was completely rebuilt in the 1880s, when the railroad's promoters decided that the building needed a much more appealing appearance and therefore significantly altered the building's design. Building upgrades were generally more subtle, and certainly less laborious. The addition of a mansard roof was especially common in Montpelier in the 1870s and '80s, for example, as the photographic evidence attests repeatedly. The Langdon building on the corner of State and Elm Streets and the Pavilion Hotel are perfect examples of that trend.

In terms of complexity, though, face-lifts paled in comparison to another 1800s Montpelier habit: the moving of buildings. Despite requiring monumental efforts and even utilizing oxen, it was clearly considered worthy again and again. There are countless examples of buildings being moved in town, from very large structures (the 1884 Golden Fleece building on Main Street, for example) to small houses. Records show that sometimes buildings were moved across town; other times it was just a building's length or two. The reasons for these relocations varied, but usually it was to make room for new construction.

A chronological analysis of Montpelier's homes shows that the city's most fervent construction decades were the 1870s, 1880s and 1890s. One period source tallied 317 Montpelier homes built between 1891 and 1902 alone. This late 1800s housing boom is consistent with a post–Civil War period of construction that occurred nationally. Another trend in home construction in Montpelier at this time was larger and more ornate residences. There were many lavish Victorian homes built in the Queen Anne, Italianate and Second Empire styles during the early portion of this period, indicating a fairly prosperous citizenry. Texts of the late 1800s corroborate this prosperity, asserting that businesses in Montpelier were thriving, for the most part. Many of the beautiful houses built by the business leaders of that time still exist.

Today Montpelier boasts the state's largest historic district. First entered into the National Register of Historic Places in 1978 and expanded in 1989 and 2008, the district now includes 576 buildings and structures in the city's downtown core and adjoining neighborhoods. The historic integrity of this district is indicated by the fact that fully 89 percent of the buildings in the district are considered "contributing" structures. The city of Montpelier, the nation's smallest capital city, has grown from a clearing in the woods at the confluence of two rivers to a vibrant and well-preserved city with buildings from a variety of periods. Photographs of those buildings and the activities surrounding them tell the story of the city's past.

Above: Montpelier was probably just over seventy years old when this view looking east was captured in the early 1860s. The town's third State House, having just recently been constructed, sits prominently on the left. The Civil War hospital was not yet built, helping to date the photo. From this perspective, the hospital would later have been visible on the hill in the background. That same hill was also the location of the 1853 and 1857 Vermont State Fairs.

Right: Taken beside one of the earliest streets in Montpelier, this image shows Hill Street in the foreground, as it descended west into downtown. The third State House is visible in the distance, just left of center.

This house was built by Jacob Davis on Elm Street in 1790. Reputed to have been the first frame house built in Montpelier, it was eventually used as a county jail until 1858, when it was moved up Elm Street.

One of the very first buildings in Montpelier (built about 1790), the Cadwell House was known primarily as a center for Montpelier social life. Its two most famous guests were President James Monroe (in 1817) and the Marquis de Lafayette (in 1825).

Images taken from both sides of State Street, and both looking toward Main Street in 1874. (Top photo) In the background is a structure known as the "arch building," probably built about 1840. In 1883, that building was destroyed to help clear the way for an easier entrance to the street that would lead up to the Seminary Hill area. Originally known as the State Street extension, this road uphill (as seen in the bottom photo) would later adopt the name East State Street. At the top of the hill is Vermont Methodist Seminary.

Only a few years after this image of Main Street was captured (in about 1880), the Blanchard Block would stand about where the photographer stood. The Unitarian church is the standout building in the center of this photo.

In this view of the east side of Main Street (from where it intersects with State), the three steeples belong to the Unitarian, the Methodist and the Congregational churches (from left to right).

This is School Street looking east in about 1880. Note the very auspicious Union School that serves as the street's dead end. Judging by maps of the time, when the school opened in 1859, it appeared to be the furthermost eastern building of the downtown area.

Taken about 1880, this photo demonstrates late 1800s southeastward town growth. The seminary on the hill (at right in background) was no longer as isolated as it had been when constructed in 1872.

James Langdon visualized this small street off Main Street as a perfect place for a shopping area. To make room for his vision, the building on the left was eventually razed, and the one on the right was moved around the corner soon after this photo was taken.

Langdon Street emerges as an early experiment in urban planning, as visualized by its namesake. James Langdon died before he saw completion of his project. Judging by this photo, it's difficult to imagine just how much more he could have done.

The Blanchard Block was designed by George H. Guernsey, the city's third mayor, and constructed in 1883. Here it is seen before its 1890 addition. (See additional photograph in color section.)

This is State Street looking toward Main Street in 1928. The building on the southwest corner of State and Main housing the Montpelier Candy Kitchen (center of photo) was about one hundred years old at the time, and it continues to stand proudly today as one of the few early survivors of many downtown fires. Notice the traffic signal in the middle of the intersection.

Although cars had clearly become the dominant mode of local transportation, as evident in this 1928 image, horses were still in the picture (so to speak).

Another view from the late 1920s, this one looking south on Main Street. The two tallest structures in this view are city hall on the left and the E.W. Bailey grain elevator in the background on the right.

Chapter 2

Civic Life

With the State House as its historical focal point, Montpelier has had a proud heritage of interesting civic buildings over its two-century history, and many of these still thrive today. The city's library, city hall, schools, post offices, courthouse, train stations, hospitals and college have all played important roles in the city's history.

Since the opening of the first State House in 1808, Montpelier's architectural identity has been dominated by the state's capitol building. The first structure was constructed on land donated by Thomas Davis, son of Montpelier's founder, and was designed by local inventor and entrepreneur Sylvanus Baldwin. Just as most of the early buildings in Montpelier were constructed of wood, so was the first State House. Unfortunately, the structure was "whittled away by legislators" and was razed in 1836. The second State House was considerably larger and more durable, thanks in large part to the $132,000 that financed its construction. Unfortunately, this much larger structure was destroyed in a spectacular fire on January 5, 1857. Montpelier's third State House, a Greek temple designed by Thomas W. Silloway, was finished in time to house the 1859 legislative session. It continues to reign today as the city's most visually striking building.

Montpelier was named the county seat in 1811. The first county courthouse was constructed on the west side of the State House and was then moved to the east side. A more substantial courthouse was constructed on the corner of State and Elm Streets in 1843, but burned to the ground during its first term. A new building on the same site was completed in 1844, and then enlarged in 1879. Within a year of that expansion, however, it suffered a fire and had to be completely reconstructed.

Although state and county government had an imposing presence in Montpelier, its local governmental functions were housed in significantly more modest quarters. Lacking its own building until 1859, the village bought the Free Church building for $2,500. Used for everything from voting to entertainment, Capital Hall was the town's main gathering area until a utilitarian armory, the Golden Fleece, was built on Main Street in 1884. Then, in 1909, Montpelier spent $170,000 to construct city hall next to the armory (which was moved farther off the street).

Another formidable structure was a grand post office and federal building on State Street. The imposing granite Romanesque edifice with its arched entrances, turrets and an impressive courtroom on the second floor came in under budget and opened to a thrilled public in 1891. The *Vermont Watchman* commented in 1893, "[It] is not only the most beautiful Federal building in the State but is, with the single exception of the

State Capitol, the finest public building in Vermont." Its perceived grandeur eventually waned, however, and the once notable structure was demolished in 1963 to make room for a more modern counterpart.

Unfortunately, Montpelier's main railroad station suffered the same fate as that of the post office. The Central Vermont Railway station had been built on State Street across the street from the Pavilion Hotel and State House. In 1880, the station was completely rebuilt and enlarged, providing an impressive entrance for visitors. In 1963, the same year the post office was demolished, the station fell victim to the wrecking ball. On the eastern side of town, the Montpelier and Wells River Railroad started using an Italianate brick structure as its station in 1882. That building stands today.

Montpelier's civic life has also included numerous school buildings. The first for which there is a photographic record was the Union School, built in 1859. This very imposing structure at the end of School Street handled the load of public school students single-handedly until 1901, when a new school opened on East State Street for the lower grades. Montpelier's inventory of school structures increased again when a new high school was built on Main Street in 1941. By the 1930s, Union School was outdated and in disrepair. Depression-era federal funds were procured and a new school, also called Union School, was built in front of the old one and opened in 1939.

Perhaps the shortest-lived civic building in town was a Civil War hospital built in 1864. Sloan Army Hospital was devoted primarily to treating soldiers from New England, and it served this purpose until several months after the war ended. Newbury Seminary then purchased land on this hill and reused some of the hospital's wards. Other buildings were divided and recycled as housing in the area that became known as Seminary Hill. The school has had various names over the years but was known as Montpelier Seminary for almost fifty years beginning in 1894. The name, ownership and organizational structure of the college would change over the years, but the one building that has always towered above all others on the site is known as College Hall, a Second Empire stalwart built in 1872.

Another seemingly permanent fixture in Montpelier is Main Street's Kellogg-Hubbard Library. When Martin and Fanny Hubbard died within months of each other in 1889, Montpelier stood to benefit greatly from their $350,000 estate. Money had been designated to construct a magnificent entrance gate to the town's Green Mount Cemetery and to have a library built. Unfortunately, the Hubbard money became tied up in litigation when Fanny Hubbard's nephew, John Hubbard, contested the will. In 1894, John Hubbard finally agreed to have the library built, and it opened two years later.

Montpelier benefited from a flurry of construction of civic buildings at the turn of the twentieth century. Between 1881 and 1911, five significant public buildings were constructed and two were expanded. Along with the Wood Gallery, Dewey Day and the capital's centennial, the period is notable for its outpouring of civic pride. Although some of Montpelier's civic buildings are sadly gone now, many of its public buildings still stand, preserving the city's architectural identity and the contributions of Montpelier residents from earlier eras.

Taken from a daguerreotype, this image is one of very few known to exist of Vermont's second State House. The imposing edifice was designed by noted architect Ammi B. Young and completed in 1837.

Despite heroic efforts by residents of Montpelier to save the building, it burned down in 1857 when a furnace overheated the floor above.

In 1886, the State House was expanded on the western side to provide more room for the State Library and Supreme Court.

A commanding presence over the village of Montpelier, Silloway's State House was taller than its predecessor, and had a dome sheathed in copper and painted red. In the foreground of this 1876 photo is a railroad bridge that would have witnessed the arrival of commerce and legislators to the city.

The third State House was rebuilt on the site of its predecessor. The massive Barre granite columns and portico were reused in its construction. Designed in part by Thomas W. Silloway, who would later also design Montpelier's Unitarian church on Main Street, this final State House opened to great acclaim in October 1859.

The State House lawn has long been a favorite spot for Montpelier residents and visitors alike. This photograph, circa 1910, shows the dome that had been gilded in 1907 to keep up with current fashion, a fence later removed for a World War II scrap metal drive and majestic elm trees. The platform at the left is believed to have been a short-lived bandstand or cistern.

Equally familiar to Montpelier residents was the first-floor corridor of the State House, with its dramatic black-and-white checkered floor, fluted iron columns, plaster coffered ceiling and portraits on the walls.

Even more exuberant was the lobby to the house chamber with patterned carpet, fancy gas-lit bronze chandeliers, double sunk diamond-shaped coffers in the ceiling and heavy drapes. A display case with flags from the Civil War was at the far end of the lobby. The revolving door was added around 1900 and removed in 1946.

A circa 1900 view from the hillside behind Haymarket Square, future site of Main Street's city hall. Haymarket Square was an early Montpelier farmers' market, but had to relinquish this site in 1909 to the hall's construction.

This photo from 1909 shows city hall on Main Street in the early stages of construction. The building to the left in the background is James French's original post office, relocated for a second time. For its final move (retaining this position today), it was also turned sideways to face East State Street, rather than Main Street.

Beset with construction delays and then needing some rework (for the buckling of a hastily laid floor, for example), city hall opened in 1911 to a delighted public. Its clock tower stands 150 feet high, once qualifying the structure as among the tallest in the state.

Montpelier's first permanent fire station (1867) sat behind a stone shed on East State Street. In 1920, the first motorized firefighting equipment was purchased by the town, and the last horse was retired in 1924, the same year that this new fire station was christened on Main Street.

Right: James French became the postmaster of Montpelier in 1861. Because he had trouble securing a location for his postal reign, he simply decided to build Montpelier's first designated post office on State Street, shown in this 1860s photo.

Below: About 1869, James Langdon bought a piece of State Street property from James French. As part of the deal, French had to move his post office building, so he relocated it to Main Street. In the area vacated by the old post office, Langdon had this building constructed, first open for business in 1874. Moved to a temporary location for a few years, the post office again took up residence in practically the exact same spot it had been earlier, but in this very different building.

Montpelier citizens were thrilled when this federal building/post office opened in 1891. It was significantly larger than any town post office preceding it, and was a source of the town's architectural pride for many years. Unfortunately, it was demolished and replaced in early 1963.

On State Street, the Bank of Montpelier (circa 1826) was sandwiched between the courthouse (1844) and James French's post office (1861), and partially blocked the turn onto Elm Street. In 1869, the bank was torn down and the post office was relocated to Main Street.

Following an expansion of the courthouse in 1879, a fire burned most of the wood detail (including the building's clock tower) in 1880. This photo from the early 1900s shows the replacement clock tower and, to the left of the courthouse, the 1891 federal building/post office.

The Vermont Central Railroad station was built on State Street in 1850, and allowed incoming passengers a very nice view of the State House as they left the station. This image, in fact, was taken from the road leading up to the State House, probably about 1870.

In 1880, the train station was rebuilt to make it more attractive (ostensibly to impress incoming legislators). Retaining only a first-floor resemblance of its original design (compare the first-floor windows and doorway to those in the earlier photo), this ornate structure eventually outlived its usefulness. By the 1940s, it was used as a bus station, and then finally demolished in 1963.

Though this particular occasion is unknown, a crowd poses for the photographer behind the rebuilt train station in the early 1880s. Note the ornate woodwork on the eaves of the building.

Right: Bystanders appear to be waiting for a train in front of the Montpelier and Wells River Railroad station on Main Street. An Italianate 1876 building first serving the railroad in 1882, this building still stands, unlike its State Street counterpart. It's been decades, though, since the last train ticket was bought here.

Below: Sloan Army Hospital, sitting on the hill just east of downtown, began operations in June 1864 and treated 1,670 soldiers before it closed in October 1865. The twenty-five buildings were arranged in "pavilion" style, described as being similar to the position of spokes on a wheel. Note the fence around the hospital, designed to keep the patients inside and the "peddlers" outside. *Photograph courtesy of UVM Department of Special Collections.*

Situated near Sloan Hospital, the arsenal buildings were constructed in 1864 to hold $600,000 worth of weapons and ammunition. This firepower was presented to Montpelier as "compensation" for the town's acceptance of the hospital. Most of the arsenal burned in September 1945, leaving only the small brick building on the right side of the photograph.

Named for its founder in 1896, Heaton Hospital was Montpelier's first hospital, and only the third in the state. Thanks mainly to personal health-related experiences, Homer W. Heaton recognized the need for medical care close to home, and contributed $30,000 to the Seminary Hill–area hospital built on the ten acres that he had acquired from the Lane Manufacturing Company.

Kinstead, the Board of Charities and Probation shelter home, was supported by many local organizations. In 1922, it took up residence in this old house on upper Main Street, overlooking Seminary Hill.

The 1840s Shepard House was moved to allow for construction of the Kellogg-Hubbard, even serving as the library while the new building was erected. Later used as a boardinghouse, the infamous old home was known as the Kellogg.

Above: The year 1896 saw the opening of the Kellogg-Hubbard Library, a $60,000 Main Street project. Not only were the construction costs covered by private funds (thanks to the Martin and Fanny Kellogg estate), but an endowment allowed the library to run without the assistance of public funds for about seventy-five years.

Left: Probably taken when the Kellogg-Hubbard Library opened in 1896, this interior photo of the building's entry shows the front desk at the left and the main reading room's fireplace in the distance. The relative calm of the reading room belied the controversy that preceded its construction. John Hubbard became a pariah to many local townspeople when he contested his aunt's will. Several local leaders filed a countersuit, and three years of battling ensued before a compromise was reached. Hubbard regained the respect and admiration of the local populace when it was discovered upon his death in 1899 that he had left a $125,000 bequest to the library, alleviating any concerns about its funding for decades to come.

The Kellogg-Hubbard librarian entertains a class of youngsters in the early 1900s.

All dressed up appropriately for Dewey Day in 1898, the "Dewey schoolhouse" on Court Street generally appeared more modest, as it does to this day.

A rare interior image of a classroom at St. Michael's School, 1905. This early Catholic school was situated behind the church on Court Street, but later found a home on Barre Street.

In 1858, Montpelier decided to consolidate its education system, thereby combining its four schools into one. The result was Union School, which opened the following year.

The Union School's eighty-year reign ended in 1939 when it was demolished in favor of a brand-new school built with federal funds. The new Union School opened the following year.

A class photo on the steps in front of Union School, probably taken about 1900.

Union School's class of 1891, the same year that annual attendance increases prompted city officials to add a large wing onto the old building.

The East State Street School was built in 1901, accommodating first, second and third graders. This May Day celebration scene was worthy of a posed photograph.

Montpelier High's class of 1930 poses on the front steps of the 1914 Main Street school.

Following the Civil War, the Newbury Seminary bought the Sloan Hospital land and buildings (some of which are on the left in this image) and completed what is now known as College Hall in 1872 (at right). Portions of some of the hospital buildings were reused as additions to residences in the area then known as Seminary Hill. After a succession of names, the school became known as the Vermont Methodist Seminary in 1888 and the Montpelier Seminary in 1894.

The dining hall for the Montpelier Seminary, with its fancy decorated ceiling and central heating stove, was probably located on the fourth floor of the main building.

In 1894, the "stepping stones to success" were shorthand (seen on the blackboard) and typewriters.

A photo of the 1913 seminary baseball team. Beginning in the late 1800s, there were several baseball teams in the area sponsored by various local organizations and businesses.

For many decades, Montpelier maintained a poor farm for indigent residents. First located in Berlin, this later building on Elm Street was expanded in 1916. After the development of statewide social services, the city sold the buildings in 1956. Only the barn (at left) still remains, now a part of the Woodbury College campus.

The Vermont Historical Society, a private nonprofit organization, has a long history of occupying space in state buildings. This is the "state cabinet," which occupied a room on the first floor of the State House, the society's third home, from 1859 until 1886.

The society's fourth home, seen here in 1918, was on the second floor of the annex built onto the western side of the State House in 1886.

Chapter 3
Economic Life

In the late eighteenth and early nineteenth centuries, Montpelier was home to many successful businesses. Most of these businesses closed a long time ago, but the business leaders of yesterday are remembered today for the names they bestowed upon the city's streets and buildings. Blanchard, Lane, Langdon, Pitkin, Baldwin, Bailey, Sabin, Taplin, Heaton and Hubbard are a few of the names of businessmen that are familiar today as street and building names. Many of these wealthy entrepreneurs not only founded their own businesses, but also served on the boards of directors of others and were present at the formation of cultural and civic organizations.

By the end of its first one hundred years, Montpelier's relative wealth was evident. In 1902, the *Vermonter*, a popular journal published in White River Junction, produced a special issue devoted to the growth of the capital city. "Montpelier is a wealthy city," it pronounced. To offer proof of this claim, the in-depth article claimed that the grand list of property valuation at the time was proportionately larger than that of any other town or city in the state. Overall, the city ranked third in the state in combined appraised value of real estate and personal property. "At the same time," the article continued, "it has the advantage of a comparatively low rate of taxation."

There were several contributing factors to Montpelier's financial health during its first century and beyond. Montpelier industrialists harnessed water power along the Winooski and North Branch Rivers; entrepreneurs established large insurance companies, beginning with the Vermont Mutual Fire Insurance Company in 1828; the railroad began servicing the town in 1849; and the granite quarries of neighboring towns provided the raw materials for finishing businesses. Montpelier also fostered a group of banks and hotels to support the economy of the city. All of the necessary ingredients for a thriving local economy were available, and Montpelier took full advantage of them.

Many of Montpelier's small shops grew up along the North Branch near the Winooski and farther upstream at the falls. This location was the site of Jacob Davis's first mill in town and was later the location of the Lane Manufacturing Company. Another group of industries evolved on the south side of the Winooski River near Main Street, the most prominent industry in this location being Montpelier Manufacturing Company and, later, the Colton Manufacturing Company. A third industrial region was on the flats of the Winooski River east of downtown, along the railroad tracks. It was here that granite sheds were built after the Civil War. Interestingly, Montpelier has even been home to several clothespin companies over the years, and one of those clothespin-producing operations faced a large grain milling business on the north side of the Winooski on Main Street. The original mill building, constructed on the riverbank in 1872, burned in 1923 and was replaced by a large concrete grain elevator that towered over that side of Main Street into the 1960s.

Though most of the larger industrial operations in Montpelier no longer exist, the city has always supported small retail establishments. The most conspicuous of these, of course, have been located on State Street and Main Street, the commercial center of the city. Even the more remote neighborhoods across the city, however, have been home to successful small enterprises for many years.

Montpelier economic life in the twentieth century featured state government and the insurance industry as its two largest forces, a fact illustrated by the presence of the large and impressive National Life home office right next door to the State House. The WPA guide to Vermont, published in 1937, noted, "At noontime and at four o'clock when the State offices and the insurance offices turn a flood of humanity into State Street, the city fairly swarms with a brief punctual life, that swiftly subsides to leave the streets quiet and empty." Montpelier has also been home to Union Mutual Insurance Co., Vermont Mutual Insurance Co. and numerous banks.

Although Montpelier's foreign-born population was ignored by the writers of the WPA guide, the city attracted a significant number of immigrants in the late nineteenth century to support its granite and manufacturing industries. In 1895, 46 percent of its population was identified by city census takers as consisting of nationalities other than American. By 1915, that number had grown to 53 percent. The largest ethnic groups were French (i.e., French-Canadian), Irish, Italian and "mixed." Many of these immigrant groups clustered around the granite sheds on Barre Street and the southeastern corner of the city, and around the Lane Company's shops in the vicinity of North Franklin Street.

As the seat of county and state government, Montpelier has always needed numerous hotels to house out-of-town visitors. The village's first tavern was built by the town's founder, Jacob Davis, across the North Branch from his home. Fittingly, the city's third hotel was built by Davis's son, Thomas Davis. Montpelier was selected as the first permanent seat of the legislature in 1805, and it was Thomas Davis who donated the land for the State House. He then built a hotel on the adjacent land, completing it in 1807, one year before the capitol was ready for occupation. The subsequent hotel on this site, the Pavilion Hotel, became known as "Vermont's Third House" because it was so popular with legislators and because so much business was conducted there. Other prominent Montpelier hotels have been the Union House, Montpelier House, Riverside and Montpelier Tavern.

Although tourism has always served as a nice boost to the local economy, it would be difficult, from a historic standpoint, to isolate one or two dominant types of industry as being the keys to Montpelier's financial success. From its beginnings, the city has maintained a fairly versatile mix of business and industry, and that versatility has allowed it to prosper through the good times and weather the bad times.

Prior to the advent of electrical refrigerators, ice was a vital part of everyday life and hence a viable business opportunity. Ice was stored in sawdust in large buildings and then delivered to homes. In this photo from the early 1900s, the owner of North Branch Ice on Cummings Street, George W. Parmenter, in the wagon at the extreme left, poses with his employees and teams. The building in this photo has long since disappeared.

The North Branch Ice delivery wagon makes its rounds along Elm Street.

Over the years, numerous stores have supplied Montpelier residents with groceries. On the corner of Elm Street, one of Montpelier's oldest streets, the Sweeney and Sweeney Cash Grocery Store served the community in the late 1800s. This building has been occupied by numerous grocery stores through the present day.

The *Argus and Patriot*, Montpelier's newspaper, was founded in 1863 by Hiram Atkins, known as the "war horse" of the Democratic Party. Here, his staff poses for a picture outside of the newspaper's offices on Main Street. The paper was managed by the Atkins family until it was sold to the *Barre Times* in 1959. This building still stands, albeit in a much altered form, and still houses an office for the paper's successor, the *Times Argus*.

The Charles H. Cross & Son Bakery was a fixture in Montpelier for 151 years. The building in this circa 1865 photograph was located at the corner of Main and School Streets next door to the Old Brick Church. The bakery was torn down when Bethany Church was built in 1868.

Near its previous building on Main Street, the Cross Bakery promoted its famous Montpelier Crackers and Betsy Ross Bread in the 1930s.

The village of Montpelier purchased this former church building on State Street in 1859 and used it for village meetings and entertainment. From the late 1800s into the early 1900s, it was known as Capital Hall. In 1897, the old hall was sold to O.R. Collins to house his carriage shop.

The impressive produce spread in front of the Frank Corry Market, a fish retailer at 128 Main Street in the 1890s. The sign indicates just how popular oysters were at the time. The storefront, next to the Union Hotel on the west side of Main Street, continued to house other food markets through the years.

This structure at 40–42 Main Street, in the French Block, has a long history of hosting various retail businesses, mostly grocery stores. In this photo from 1907, Marvin & Sherburne occupied the space. Note the posters advertising "Forepaugh & Ellis Brothers Circus coming to Montpelier on August 4." (See photo in Chapter 6.)

By the time this photo was taken in 1937, First National Stores had taken over the storefront at 40–42 Main Street. Also in the French Block were W.H. Fishman & Co. "5 cents to $1.00" store, E.L. Segel Clothing Co. and Berry & Jones groceries. *Photo courtesy of Vermont State Archives.*

This building was constructed as the post office on State Street by James French in 1861. (See Chapter 2.) After its move to Main Street about 1870, the building housed Alfred L. Carlton's dry goods business. Note that a mansard roof has been added, in comparison to the flat roof on the post office.

Main Street's Blanchard Harness shop seems just large enough to support the enormous billboard on top of it. This building on the east side of Main Street near city hall still stands, although the large display windows have been covered over.

Small businesses run by mechanics and various smiths lined the east side of Elm Street, circa 1890. At one time this street was the industrial heart of the village. The corner of the Langdon Block on Main Street can be seen at the right edge of this photo.

An 1896 view of the backs of the shops on Elm Street shows how close these buildings were built to the river. These businesses almost assuredly took advantage of the North Branch for the manufacturing process and waste disposal.

Located on the Berlin side of the Winooski River, slightly removed from the retail and commercial centers of the city, was a large row of industrial buildings with their backs against the Winooski River and their entrances along the very narrow Berlin Street. Many of the structures dated back to the 1850s. They began to be eliminated one by one beginning in the 1930s, until the very last remnants of the set were taken down in the 1950s when this street, renamed Memorial Drive, was widened considerably. Prior to the 1850s, there had been several mills located along the river here, including a cotton mill owned by Sylvanus Baldwin, the architect of the first State House and the Red Arch Bridge. The State House dome, before it was gilded, and a group of workers can be seen in the distance.

The row of industrial buildings along the Winooski River was anchored by the Colton Manufacturing Company at the far left. This photo, probably taken in the mid-1890s, again demonstrates the importance of water to the industrial growth of the city. The Red Arch Bridge is at the left edge of the photograph.

Factory workers at the Colton Manufacturing Company pose for a group photo, probably taken about 1910. The plant employed about seventy men at the time of this photo, so this crew doesn't represent the company's entire workforce. Makers of saddlery hardware and one of the largest nickel- and silver-plating operations in the country (according to period sources), the company actually dated back to 1858, but occasionally experienced new ownership. Originally Fisher and Stratton, then Fisher and Colton, then Johnson and Colton and finally simply Colton Manufacturing Company, this successful venture also had a branch office in Chicago.

Downstream from the Colton Manufacturing Company, the very industrial-looking three-story building on the right was where Greene's Syrup of Tar was manufactured. Similar to other products of its time, Greene's was a medicinal concoction reputed to cure coughing. It also contained opium, not an uncommon medicinal ingredient one hundred years ago.

The northern bank of the Winooski River just east of the city held railroad yards and industrial buildings of various sorts. This view was taken from the E.W. Bailey grain elevator on Main Street in 1929.

This view of the intersection of Northfield Street and Berlin Street was taken from the Bailey grain elevator in 1929. Prior to 1898, this side of the river was within the Berlin town limits. The odd-looking rooftop contraption in the lower right of the photo is a portion of a giant clothespin, marking the U.S. Clothespin Company building. This was the same factory building that had once housed Colton Manufacturing. The road in front of this building was still dirt at this time.

Andrew and Susie Berganti's gas station on Berlin Street in 1928. This building can be seen to the left in the image at the top of the page. This section of the city included a small grocery store, a scrap yard and small manufacturing companies, in addition to residences.

Montpelier's granite sheds were located along the railroad tracks toward the eastern end of Barre Street. Immigrant families lived nearby on surrounding streets. The Granite Street bridge, built in 1902, can be seen in the lower portion of the photograph.

Timothy Kelleher's granite workers pose just outside the Montpelier Granite Works building in the late 1870s. Kelleher is the third man from the left in the front row, wearing a white cap and extending his leg. The edges of the Arch Bridge and the Bailey gristmill can be seen on either side of the brick building. The Montpelier & Wells River Railroad later took over this building.

A horseshoe-shaped granite shed, owned by a succession of companies over the years, was at the eastern end of the group of sheds located on Barre Street. Homes along Sibley Avenue looked out over the sheds. Montpelier Seminary is at the top of the hill.

Founded in 1892, the granite business of Harry J. Bertoli was located on the west side of Pioneer Street. Bertoli, who arrived in America in 1888, produced some of the most notable monuments in Montpelier's Green Mount Cemetery, including the famous "Little Margaret" Pitkin sculpture. *Photo courtesy of Sandra Collins.*

The Montpelier Slate Company was founded by Charles T. Sabin in 1882 and was located on forty acres of land on the eastern side of the city. The company employed thirty-five men and produced black slate exclusively for roofing. Impressions left by the explosives used in mining the slate are visible today, though the tracks seen in these photos have long since disappeared. The business remained somewhat profitable until the late 1890s. The Montpelier Slate Company sold all of its equipment at a foreclosure auction in 1903 when the company disbanded. The quarry and slate remnants are still visible today.

Upstream from the small shops that lined the banks of the North Branch along Elm Street in the historic center of the village was a much larger enterprise, Lane Manufacturing Company. Most of these buildings were practically new when this photo of the company's buildings was taken in 1868. Though the company is long gone, a few of the twelve buildings comprising the business during its heyday continue to survive, thanks mainly to refurbishing efforts in the 1980s.

One of the few brick buildings in the Lane Manufacturing complex. Dennis Lane began to build his empire when he bought a small foundry from Alfred Wainwright in 1863. Two years later, Colonel Perley P. Pitkin joined forces with Lane, and James Brock came on board as another co-owner in 1873, when the operation became the Lane Manufacturing Company. By 1890, selling its patented lever set sawmills in seven states, the company employed about one hundred men. Unfortunately, Lane died in 1888 at the height of the company's growth and profitability.

The management team of the Montpelier & Barre Light & Power Company poses for a photograph at a convention in Swampscott, Massachusetts, in 1925. The "Montpelier Indians" (which is how the old photo caption referred to them) were possibly also trying to promote another successful Montpelier product, the clothespin. *Photo courtesy of Vermont State Archives.*

"Collars and cuffs are laundried in the most perfect style, and particular attention is devoted to shirts and gentleman's underwear" is how a book about Vermont businesses described Montpelier Steam Laundry's virtues in 1891. This photo, taken about that time, shows the proud crew of this establishment. Originally located at 3 Barre Street, the business moved into the Golden Fleece building around the corner (to Main Street) in the late 1880s. It's possible that the man at the far left is Fred Whitcomb, the proprietor. In 1896, Whitcomb's successful venture moved to a block he built across the street at 28 Main.

Montpelier has long been home to successful insurance companies. Vermont Mutual Fire Insurance Company, founded in 1828 by Daniel Baldwin, was the first insurance company in Montpelier and one of the first mutual insurance companies in the nation. Its headquarters, and now its fourth home office (seen above in 1909), was located on State Street. In this photograph a meatpacking business can be seen on Taylor Street and a grocery store was located down State Street next to the American House.

National Life Insurance Company, founded in 1848 by Dr. Julius Y. Dewey, has had seven home offices in Montpelier. By the early 1920s, the company had outgrown its fifth home, an 1891 Romanesque building at 116 State Street (see photograph in color section) and built a new office building at 133 State Street (see photograph of completed building in color section). Neoclassical in design, and sitting just west of the State House, it was intended to create symmetry with the similarly neoclassical Supreme Court building that sat on the other side of the State House. This five-story edifice was originally planned to be seven stories, but it was decided that the extra two floors would not balance well with the rest of the "State House quadrangle." Cram & Ferguson of Boston designed the new building while S. Edwin Tobey of Boston had designed the previous home office; a Boston contractor built both buildings.

The interior of 133 State Street, National Life's new home in 1921, had an ornately detailed lobby and other luxurious appointments. The building was intended to have a future wing to the west of this lobby, making the building symmetrical, but in 1959 the company built a new home on a different site rather than expand this building.

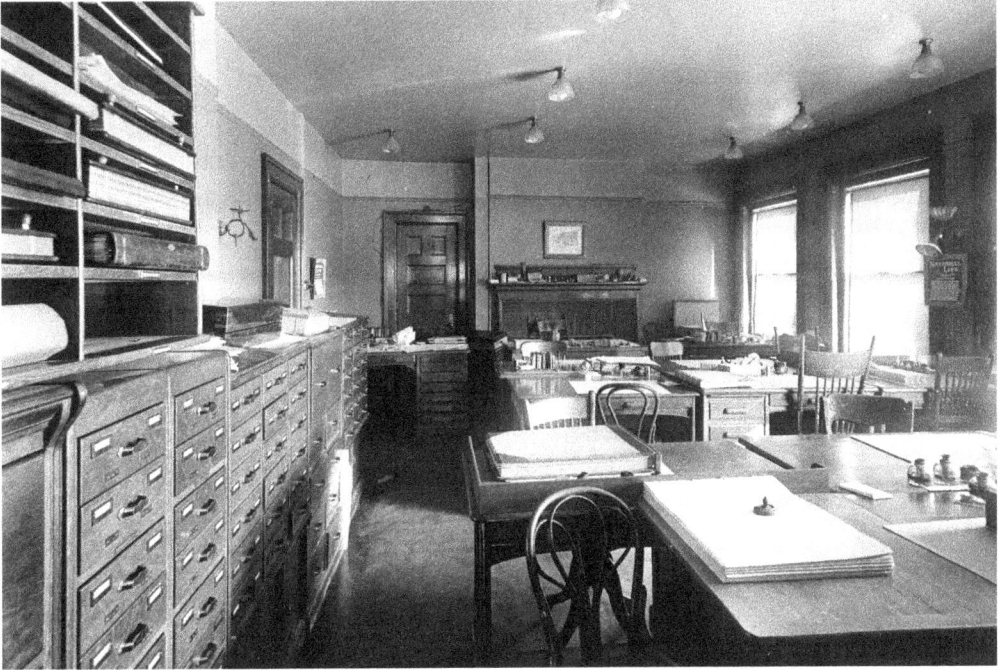

Taken about 1902, this photo shows a very quiet Actuarial Department at National Life in the company's 1891–1922 brick and brownstone office building at 116 State Street.

Workers in the Printing Room at National Life pause from their duties for a quick pose in 1913.

The Montpelier Savings Bank occupied a prominent location at the corner of State and Main Streets. This colorful building, composed of red brick and light gray granite, was built by James R. Langdon as the flagship of his urban planning project. This photo was probably taken about 1900, soon after the bank opened.

Just around the corner, located at 13 State Street, was the Montpelier National Bank, marked by a distinctive white marble façade and a freestanding clock at the edge of the street. The bank was founded in 1865 by James R. Langdon and others.

1. The city of Montpelier as seen from behind the State House looking east toward the Main Street bridge. The old Catholic church with the double white steeples still stands next to the capitol, while the new church on Barre Street can be seen in the distance.

2. The city of Montpelier as seen from the Catholic cemetery above Main Street looking west. The old Union School is on the left, while far in the distance, beyond the State House, is Redstone, the home of Professor John W. Burgess, on Terrace Street.

3. *View of the village of Montpelier taken from Mill Point in Berlin* by Mrs. S.I. Watrous, from James Whitelaw's 1824 map of Vermont. This view shows the first State House and a courthouse to the left of the capitol building.

4. The third State House had a red dome prior to its gilding in 1907.

5. A later version of the Watrous illustration from the 1851 Whitelaw map of Vermont. In this view the second State House has been built, and the Catholic church is now shown to the right of the capitol building.

6. The third State House was updated with gold on its dome in 1907. This view includes an iron fence that was removed later. All that remains today of this fence are the two biggest pillars in this image.

7. Although labeled "Lower State Street," this postcard shows the end of the trolley line at the corner of Bailey Avenue and State Street. This view is looking east toward the State House and downtown. The street to the left is Bailey Avenue. Bailey Avenue was not extended across State Street and the Winooski River until 1958, soon after the high school was built.

8. With large, impressive houses on one side of the street and the winding Winooski River on the other, lower State Street was an impressive entrance to the city from the west until the interstate opened in 1960, changing the approach to the city forever.

9. State Street in the early twentieth century featured brick buildings that are familiar today, along with trolley tracks that were removed after the 1927 flood.

10. These are two of the many trade cards issued by Montpelier businesses in the late nineteenth and early twentieth centuries. The trade card at the left was issued by the paper box factory located in the brick building at the head of State Street, as shown in the previous postcard.

11. This view of the 1883 Blanchard Block at the heart of Montpelier's downtown shows the building's 1890 addition constructed to house the hall of the local post of the Grand Army of the Republic, a Civil War veterans' group. Although this building has changed little over the years, awnings are no longer used by the store owners on the first floor.

THE PLACE WHERE A CHILD CAN BUY AS CHEAP AS A MAN,

IS AT

PUTNAM & MARVIN'S,

French's Block, **GROCERS,** Montpelier,

SOUTH MAIN ST., VERMONT,

WHERE YOU CAN ALWAYS FIND

A FULL LINE OF GROCERIES,

CROCKERY AND GLASSWARE.

FINE TEAS A SPECIALTY.

Don't Lose this Card; it is worth a **DOLLAR** to you.

[OVER]

12. This punch card was issued by Putnam & Marvin's, one of a long line of grocers that occupied a store at 40–42 Main Street, across the street from city hall. When customers purchased twenty dollars worth of merchandise the store would give them "one dollar in goods free of charge."

13. Haymarket Square, circa 1905, before the construction of city hall.

14. In 1909, Haymarket Square was filled in with the construction of a new city hall designed in the Italian Renaissance style. The firehouse was not built to the north of city hall until 1924. The Golden Fleece building, constructed in 1884 as an armory near the street, was moved back to make way for the city hall and stood to the right of the municipal building until 1974. Over the years, this seemingly small building housed a bowling alley and skating rink, as well as several printing businesses. On Dewey Day in 1899, it was also said to have served as an auditorium that held about two thousand people.

15. The Unitarian church, designed by State House architect Thomas W. Silloway, stands conspicuously on the west side of Main Street in this early 1900s view.

16. A fall view of the Kellogg-Hubbard Library, captured shortly after it was built in 1894. At the right, the Bethany Church steeple pierces a colorful sky.

17. Heaton Hospital is in the background of this early 1900s postcard. Liberty Street is in the foreground. A building is under construction at the lower left of this view.

18. A much closer view of Montpelier's Heaton Hospital. As this image shows, the hospital was expanded several times after the central structure was built in 1898. The complex eventually included a nurses' home built across the street in 1925. The Heaton Hospital and the Barre Hospital merged in 1968 to become the Central Vermont Hospital.

19. Montpelier's Union School stood at the far end of School Street with its back toward the lower slopes of Seminary Hill. It housed both the high school and grammar school. The structure was replaced by a new Union School in 1939, with its front door reoriented to the north side of the building on Park Street.

20. The East State Street School was constructed in 1901 to accommodate the first three grades, thus leaving more room for the upper grades, including high school, in the Union School.

21. By 1914, the school district needed more space, so this high school was constructed on Main Street. It served in this capacity until 1956, when a new high school was built on Langdon Field and the upper elementary grades were moved into this building.

22. The Vermont Conference Seminary and Female College moved to Montpelier in 1868, and in 1872 the organization completed this landmark building. This Methodist school went through numerous name changes; it was Montpelier Seminary from 1894 until 1941, then Vermont Junior College and Vermont College in 1958.

23. The Montpelier House stood on the south side of State Street from 1826 until 1932 under the ownership of a long list of proprietors. The YMCA building, home of the Wood Art Gallery, can be seen at the far left of this picture.

24. In 1932, the old Montpelier House was replaced by the Montpelier Tavern, seen here soon after it opened. Later, the YMCA building was demolished, and the Tavern was enlarged to include stores and offices.

THE FORMAL OPENING

OF

The New Pavilion

MONTPELIER, VT.,

WILL OCCUR ON

TUESDAY EVENING, FEB. 22, 1876.

Your company with ladies is respectfully solicited.

Return checks given over Central Vt. and M. & W. R. R.

BILL, $5.00 PER COUPLE.

T. O. BAILEY, PROPRIETOR.

Polands' Print, Montpelier.

25. This invitation, bordered with gold, was distributed by Theron O. Bailey to celebrate the opening of the newly erected Pavilion Hotel in 1876. Despite the fact that the country was in a recession, 325 tickets were sold to guests from Vermont and neighboring states. Dancing lasted until 5:30 the following morning.

26. The Pavilion Hotel on State Street did not receive its mansard roof until 1888, when new owner Jesse S. Viles Jr. updated the structure.

27. National Life's fifth home office building was this impressive red stone Romanesque building on State Street across the street from the Pavilion Hotel and the State House.

28. In 1921, National Life moved down the street to its sixth home office, a 106,000-square-foot building utilizing Barre granite and featuring interiors by the Vermont Marble Company.

29. After the Montpelier and Wells River Railroad established its line from Montpelier to Barre in 1889, granite sheds were built in the eastern end of the city along Barre Street. They were a substantial part of Montpelier's economy, employing scores of immigrants who lived in the neighborhood and elsewhere in the city.

30. Green Mount Cemetery, located on the western side of the city, is a showcase for the artistry of some of Montpelier's most skilled stone carvers and a resting place for some of its most prominent citizens. The cemetery was dedicated in 1855. The original iron gate was replaced by a marble chapel and entrance arch built in 1906 and partially funded by a gift of John E. Hubbard, the benefactor of the Kellogg-Hubbard Library and Hubbard Park.

31. This farm on the western edge of town on today's Three Mile Bridge Road was owned by one of the successful Bailey brothers. The eldest, J. Warren, was a merchant, grain dealer and holder of many city offices. His brother, Charles W., sold horses, cattle and sheep in the Boston market. The other brothers were Edward W. Bailey, who ran a successful grain milling operation in downtown Montpelier, and Theron O., who owned the Pavilion Hotel.

32. The Winooski River diverges from the railroad tracks in this approach into Montpelier from the west.

Just down the street at 45 State Street was another bank, Capital Savings. Founded as the First National Bank in 1864, the bank first shared this building, constructed by James R. Langdon in 1874, with the post office and other businesses. The original building had a flat roof and little ornamentation. Toward the end of the nineteenth century, a mansard roof with round dormers was added to update the building. This photo shows the building under renovation following the 1927 flood.

The newly redesigned Langdon Block is seen here in 1930. The street-level façade of the building was clad in granite, an appropriate symbol for the economic stability that the bank represented.

Montpelier's landmark hotel had origins dating back to 1807, when the first version was built on this State Street site by a son of Montpelier town founder Jacob Davis. Named the Davis Tavern, it was sold in 1827 to Mahlon Cottrill, who had an economic interest in all nine stage lines that served Montpelier. Cotrill doubled the building's size and added covered piazzas, renaming it the Pavilion Hotel. In this photo from about 1870, the Catholic church can be seen on Court Street.

Sold in 1874 to Theron O. Bailey, the Pavilion Hotel was torn down and rebuilt as a ninety-room luxury hotel, with much of the building material coming from its predecessor.

After Jesse Sumner Viles Jr. purchased the building in 1886, it received another makeover, including the addition of a mansard roof in 1888 that covered thirty-five additional rooms. By the 1960s, the old building was in major disrepair, and the state purchased it in 1966. After a nationally publicized debate as to what should be done with it, a decision was made to have it reconstructed once more. Photos and measurements were taken prior to the hotel's demolition, and then work was begun on the Pavilion's reconstruction. Again incorporating recycled construction materials, it reopened primarily as an office building in 1971 to an excited city.

This was the third Union House, located on the southwest corner of Main and School Streets to serve Montpelier visitors, and it was obviously a popular destination when this 1880s photo was taken. The previous two Union Houses had both burned down, the first in 1834 and the second in 1859. This third (and final) structure lasted longer than its two predecessors combined, but fire finally did it in too, on March 1, 1929.

Behind the Union House, just off School Street near the North Branch, were the hotel's stables.

John Davis had the Montpelier House constructed on State Street in 1826. It survived many floods and fires, and managed to retain this look for over one hundred years before finally being reconstructed as the Montpelier Tavern in 1932. In this late nineteenth-century photograph, an undertaking establishment and furniture store can been seen next door, and the train station is in the background.

The thoroughly modern Montpelier Tavern of the 1930s was flanked by a service station on the west and the YMCA building on the east. The hotel was expanded to the east in 1966 to include stores and offices.

The very spiffy coffee shop of the Tavern was justifiably showcased in this photo from 1932, the year the building was reconstructed, renamed and reopened. *Photo courtesy of Vermont State Archives.*

Another popular guest house on State Street, the Riverside Inn was built in the mid-1800s. Located across the street from the sixth National Life home office, its popularity among tourists waned by the 1940s, and the building's owners sold it to the state. In 1947, the state tore it down so that the brick Queen Anne–style Edward Dewey house could be moved to the property.

The Toy Town Cabins and Tea Room were constructed in the early 1930s, just west of the Green Mount Cemetery, for the pleasure of tourists arriving to, or departing from, the capital city along Route 2. In the 1940s, a scale model of the third State House was added to the grounds and became the central attraction at this roadside cluster of tourist cabins. The model was commissioned by the Montpelier Chamber of Commerce and built by A.G. Baird and his crew for the opening of the Lake Champlain Bridge in 1929, the same year it was pulled through the streets of Montpelier in an American Legion parade.

Chapter 4

Bridges, Roads and Rails

For the early settlers of Montpelier, even traveling within the confines of downtown could sometimes be a challenge. The rivers were a daily obstacle, mainly because the early bridges traversing them weren't very reliable. Flooding was all too common, and when the rivers became too high, the bridges (the vast majority of them covered) were often swept away.

From the late 1790s until 1826, the Main Street crossing over the Winooski was the site of a series of bridges, each succumbing to the current of a swollen river. There are a few documented instances of people who were so anxious to cross during these non-bridged intervals that they braved the dangerous currents anyway. Their small boats were no match for the current, and they were carried downstream instead. Two people even drowned attempting to cross during a storm.

It was in 1826, however, that Sylvanus Baldwin taught Montpelier an interesting lesson. Baldwin, a local inventor and architect who designed the first State House, devised a bridge that wouldn't be supported by trestles in the water, effectively making it immune to raging floodwaters. Local skeptics mocked him, fully expecting failure, but his covered bridge (known as the Old Red Arch) lasted over seventy years.

The river crossings were Montpelier's most notable transportation hurdles locally in the town's early years. For longer commutes and the import and export of goods, the stagecoach was commonly used in the beginning of the nineteenth century.

It was the advent of the railroad, however, that allowed local businesses to flourish. After a rocky start in 1835, the Vermont Central Railroad began serving Montpelier in 1849, providing a gateway to expanding national markets. The Central Vermont's tracks entered from the western side of town and utilized rail yards near Taylor Street. In 1873, the Montpelier and Wells River Railroad opened rail operations in Montpelier, improving the city's access to the granite quarries to the east.

The next significant transportation upgrade after the appearance of trains in Montpelier was the trolley. Arriving in 1898, courtesy of the Barre & Montpelier Traction Company, the street railway was used by residents to get around Montpelier, to take excursions to nearby Dewey Park or Inter-City Park in Berlin and to commute to Barre eight miles to the southeast. The trolley tracks were laid right in the middle of designated Montpelier's streets, a seemingly innocuous location at the time. At five cents per ride, it was a wonderfully convenient way to get around.

Unfortunately, the trolley was eventually upstaged and crowded out by the automobile. Cars were owned by Montpelier's wealthiest citizens at first, and then began to spread to more of the local populace (aided by Henry Ford's assembly line innovations that made them much cheaper for Americans). The introduction of cars onto Montpelier roads in the early 1900s—where horse-drawn carriages, the trolley and pedestrians were already competing for space—made for an ever-growing concern of street congestion. The quick evolution of transportation technology didn't allow for local governing bodies to anticipate the potential pitfalls of so many ways and speeds to move around.

The messy combination of local transportation eventually resolved itself. By the 1920s, the proliferation of cars and trucks had made horse-drawn vehicles almost obsolete. The trolley was suffering from competition from cars, buses and the Montpelier & Wells River, which could take passengers to more remote locations such as Groton for recreation and leisure. The flood of 1927 sealed the trolley's fate. It undermined the traction company's tracks and destroyed the Pioneer Street bridge; trolleys were not seen on the streets of Montpelier or Barre after 1927.

Although methods of transportation have changed over time, the need to make river crossings has remained a constant in Montpelier's history. The city's early collection of covered bridges was gradually replaced by steel truss bridges beginning in 1898, when the Old Red Arch Bridge was replaced by a modern truss bridge. Many of the city's remaining wooden bridges were wiped out by the 1927 flood. The replacement bridges were constructed quickly and efficiently from steel. Unfortunately, many of these steel bridges, with their structures exposed to the elements, are now showing signs of deterioration.

The covered bridge is only one of several stationary elements now gone from the streets of Montpelier. The toll collectors who watched over the bridges that allowed visitors into downtown were eliminated about 175 years ago. (At one time, a small fee had to be paid by anyone entering Montpelier.) No longer does the town furnish wooden planking for pedestrians to cross Main and State. (Montpelier's "Annual Report" always specified the amount of money the town spent on this planking.) Other elements that have disappeared from the local streetscape are the permanent traffic cone in the middle of the intersection of State and Main, the teardrop streetlights of the 1940s and street signs of all descriptions. For pedestrians and commuters alike, transportation within the small city's limits has changed considerably over the course of Montpelier's history. Only a few of the once prominent transportation relics survive.

Looking toward the Unitarian church (in the background on the right), this 1870s image illustrates the usefulness of sleighs for hauling in the winter.

An effective way to deal with snow before the advent of motorized vehicles was to pack it down and sled over it. This giant roller was so heavy it required a team of horses to haul it. Here, it takes care of the area in front of the Pavilion Hotel.

An obviously crowded group of coach passengers stops to pose for a photograph. Clearly, those on top didn't desire to disembark for the occasion.

College students rented this coach from the Pavilion Hotel livery, and the deal included John Quincy Adams (at left) as their driver. Adams, a well-respected Montpelierite, ran the hotel's livery for many years. Judging by the fact that he didn't want to face the camera, or even strike more of a pose for this staged shot, we're left to wonder how he felt about this particular assignment.

Elm Street traffic in the late 1800s.

A very posed John Quincy Adams stands at left in front of a stagecoach and its potential riders. This photo was taken at Adams's livery behind the Pavilion, and dates from about 1885.

Track for the "electric road" (the period term for trolley tracks) was laid in 1898. In this photo, a line of workers digging and placing ties has turned the corner of Main and State Streets.

Probably taken on a late fall day sometime in the early 1900s, this State Street photo shows a Barre & Montpelier trolley in the distance, having just passed underneath the large, bare elm trees on the right. Almost all of Montpelier's elm trees would eventually be decimated by Dutch elm disease.

The Barre and Montpelier Traction company began accepting riders on June 29, 1898. The main line started in front of the State House (at Bailey Avenue), and went to the Granite Bridge, South Main Street, Barre. This approximately seven-mile trip had five steam railroad grade crossings on its route.

One line of the trolley went from Barre Street, to Sibley Avenue, to Sabin Street, to Kemp Street, to College Street. The line culminated at Woodrow Avenue near Heaton Hospital in the Seminary Hill area.

The Arthur Tandy, a "Forney engine," steamed in and out of Montpelier for many years. A workhorse of the Central Vermont Railroad, it was primarily a recreational train, carrying passengers to Canada, St. Albans and New York.

This photo from about 1910 demonstrates the omnipresence of the railroad in Montpelier. These tracks represent several railroad companies that operated in the area, and the structures are typical engine houses, some of which were used for assembling the rail cars.

Dean K. Lillie glances at the camera from in front of his College Street home. Possibly either on his way to work or just arriving home in this image, this mayor of Montpelier held the position from 1924 until 1926.

L. Bart Cross and his family had their chauffeur pause in front of their School Street home for this early 1900s photo. Note that the driver's seat is on the right.

A profile of Sylvanus Baldwin's Red Arch Bridge in 1897, not long before its demise. The barely perceptible text on its railing is an advertisement for the "Forepaugh and Sells Brothers" Circus coming to town. The building in the background is the Bailey gristmill.

Carriage traffic on the Red Arch Bridge, looking south, probably about 1890. The E.W. Bailey Feed & Grist Mill (on the right) burned down in 1923.

Sylvanus Baldwin built the Red Arch Bridge in 1826, and it stood over the Winooski significantly longer than any of its predecessors, until 1898. The bridge connected what was technically Berlin (on the left side of the photo) to Montpelier's Main Street. Extrapolating from a comment in the Montpelier Annual Report of 1897, the respected old bridge's destruction was probably partly due to the concern that the bridge would not be strong enough to support the "electric road" (or trolley) coming soon. Though the trolley didn't ultimately utilize this route, the bridge was nevertheless replaced. (The same issue was raised concerning Montpelier's Rialto Bridge.) This 1886 photo shows several people examining what was most likely a fairly typical winter ice buildup.

The Red Arch Bridge was replaced by a steel truss bridge in 1898. The narrow road on the left is Winooski Avenue, which would eventually be widened considerably and renamed Memorial Drive in the mid-1950s.

A sweeping town view taken just above the Taylor Street Bridge. Note what appear to be picnickers in the foreground. It was very easy to have a hillside, unobstructed view of Montpelier in the late 1800s due to the heavy deforestation.

Facing the north end of the Taylor Street Bridge. The heavily advertised Sparks Circus was obviously a summer headliner in this photo, probably taken in 1921. This circa 1850 bridge would be washed away in rising floodwaters six years later and be replaced in 1929.

A Parker truss bridge replaced its predecessor on Taylor Street in 1929. This photo was probably taken soon after its construction.

Following the 1927 flood, there was a torrent of steel bridge building activity in Montpelier (as there was all over the state). Many of the state's bridges during this period were constructed by the American Bridge Company. No exception, here is the Langdon Street Bridge, as viewed from the Rialto Bridge (State Street).

Though the origin of its name is unknown, the Sand Bottom Bridge stood until October 1869, when it was swept away by what was then Montpelier's most devastating flood. As it floated down the river, it refused to go quietly, taking two other bridges with it. An eventual replacement was constructed and reflected its later-named location—the Cummings Street Bridge.

The Spring Street Bridge under construction. The smokestacks and a roof with cupola from the Lane Shops can be seen in the distance.

Chapter 5

Religious Life

Historian Daniel Pierce Thompson, writing in 1860, observed that by 1830 Montpelier had been transformed from industriousness and orderliness of the first settlers to a state of "moral deterioration." He wrote, "The taverns became common and constant resorts, inviting to idleness, money spending, and all sorts of dissipation… Rum drinking increased…gambling was a common practice…while the Sabbaths were generally desecrated by horse racing, match shooting, street games, holly day amusements, visiting and pleasure parties." Into this morass of depravity, according to Thompson, strove "a moral Hercules," Reverend Chester Wright.

Wright was the first pastor of the village of Montpelier's Congregational church and for a long time the only minister in town. He came to Montpelier in 1808 and built an impressive house on the western end of town, for many years the last structure in Montpelier on the road to Waterbury. Wright served until 1830, when he was removed for his strong opposition to Free Masonry. Wright's first services were held in the Montpelier Academy at the corner of Main and Spring Streets and in the State House. In 1820, the Congregationalists built the first church in what is now the city of Montpelier. Located on Main Street at the corner of School Street, the structure eventually became known as the Old Brick Church. It was here that the legislature met after the second State House burned in 1853.

The first religious group in the town of Montpelier was the Society of Friends, or Quakers, who formed a group as early as 1795. The group's first meetinghouse, however, was not in the village itself, but in the surrounding countryside. The town was also visited by Methodist circuit riders beginning in 1795. The Free Will Baptists, a group more closely aligned with the Universalists than with Baptists, had a presence in Montpelier as early as 1806 in the person of the first town clerk and ordained minister, Ziba Woodworth.

After the Congregational church was built in 1820, the other denominations followed in rapid succession leading up to the Civil War. In 1826, the Methodists built their first meetinghouse, a classic white New England structure, in Montpelier Center (now part of the town of East Montpelier). In 1837, a new Methodist church was constructed down in the village on Court Street, near Elm Street. This new structure, while also wooden, was more modest than the traditional meetinghouse in the Center.

A group broke off from the First Congregational Society and founded the Second Congregational Church, or Free Church, in 1835. They built a church building on State Street across from the courthouse but dissolved in 1848.

The Episcopalians were the next denomination to build a house of worship in Montpelier. After meeting in the Methodist meetinghouse on Court Street, they built their first structure, Christ Church, a wooden Gothic structure, on State Street in 1842. Eight years later, the Roman Catholic Church purchased the old courthouse on the east side of the State House and converted it into a place of worship. The small building served the congregation until a new, considerably larger structure, St. Augustine's, was built and dedicated in 1859.

A flurry of church building also followed the Civil War. The Independent Meeting House Society, under the leadership of a Unitarian minister, dedicated the Church of the Messiah in 1866. In 1868, the Episcopalians built a new, granite church, still called Christ Church, opposite the post office. The Old Brick Church had become dilapidated by 1858, but it was not until the Episcopalians completed their church that the Congregationalists completed their own large Gothic stone church, called Bethany. Around the corner from the imposing Congregational church in a residential neighborhood near the Union School, the Baptists built their new church. The small wooden building with exquisite Gothic details was completed in 1873.

Back on Main Street, the Methodists were also building a new brick church. Begun in 1868, the year that the Episcopalians and Congregationalists completed their churches, Trinity Methodist Church took six years to complete. It would hold seven hundred people, more than twice the number the Baptists could accommodate.

The Roman Catholics, following the pattern of so many of the other Montpelier denominations, again started planning for a new church. They outgrew their 1859 brick church on Court Street and bought land a little closer to many of their communicants on Barre Street. The cornerstone of a new St. Augustine's was laid by Bishop Louis DeGroesbriand in 1892. The first service in the new granite church was held in 1903. A steeple on the east side of the church and a tower on the west side were planned for the large structure, but were never built. St. Michael's School was opened in 1874 near the original St. Augustine's and a newer school was constructed on Barre Street in 1931.

Other religious groups have also served Montpelier's population. The First Church of Christ, Scientist, was organized in the capital city in 1905 and held services in different locations until 1972, when their church was dedicated. Jews have lived in Montpelier since the late nineteenth century, and in 1913 a Jewish congregation was organized. The following year, this congregation purchased a residence on Harrison Avenue and converted it into a synagogue known as Beth Jacob, named in honor of Jacob Yett, who was killed when ice fell off the roof of Union School.

The period after 1940 (the final year of the photos included in this book) has seen many architectural changes to Montpelier's religious institutions. The most notable of these are probably the demolition and reconstruction of most of the Bethany Church in the late 1950s and the removal of the Christ Church steeple in 1963. During the second half of the twentieth century, numerous other locations have been used as houses of worship and contemplation by a variety of organizations.

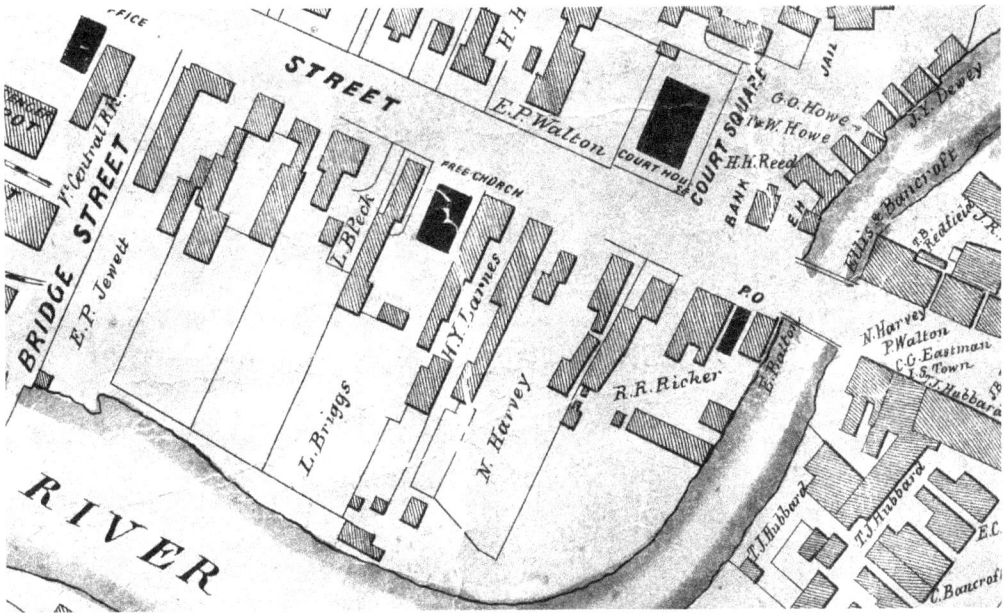

This 1853 map of Montpelier shows the location of the Free Church (just above the center of the image), one of Montpelier's early churches, located on State Street across from the courthouse and near the post office. The building was constructed by the Second Congregational Church, which had organized in 1835 and dissolved in 1848. In 1859, the Free Church building became Capital Hall, the seat of city government.

Montpelier's 1877 skyline was dominated by Bethany Church (center). Three other churches can be seen in this view: the old Methodist church on Court Street (far left), Church of the Messiah (center, just beyond Bethany) and the new Trinity Methodist Church on Main Street (right). The buildings in the foreground were located on East State Street.

Above left: The Old Brick Church, the first permanent meetinghouse in Montpelier, was built on Main Street near School Street in 1820.

Above right: The interior of the Bethany Church, seen here circa 1880, was as impressive as its exterior (next photo).

In 1868, led by the church's longtime pastor Reverend W.H. Lord, the Montpelier Congregationalists built a colorful Gothic church on the site of their former church and the Cross Bakery building next door. An impressive rose window was installed over the three arched entrances at the School Street end of the sanctuary.

In 1826, the Methodists finished a meetinghouse in Montpelier Center. Eleven years later, they built this church on Court Street in the rapidly growing village.

By 1868, the Methodists were ready to build another church, this time on Main Street. Trinity Methodist Church took six years to complete, but when it was finished in 1874, it could seat seven hundred worshipers.

Episcopalians organized in Montpelier in 1840. Their first services were held in the Methodist meetinghouse on Court Street. In 1842, a small wooden Episcopal church (above) on State Street at the foot of Western (now Governor Aiken) Avenue was dedicated. The congregation grew and, in 1867–68, a Gothic church built of Barre and Berlin granite (left) was built farther down State Street opposite the courthouse. The architect of the church, which cost $30,000 to build, was J.J. Randall of Rutland.

In 1850, the Roman Catholic Church purchased the old courthouse next to the State House (seen here on the left) and remodeled it as a place of worship. In 1859, St. Augustine's, a new brick edifice next door, was dedicated.

The cornerstone for the new St. Augustine's on Barre Street was ceremoniously laid on July 4, 1892. The church's steeples were never built. This view was taken in 1929 from the E.W. Bailey grain elevator.

A Universalist meetinghouse, known as the Brick Church, was dedicated in East Montpelier in 1838. Other groups loosely associated with the Unitarian and Universalist denominations met in various locations in the growing village. In 1864, the Montpelier Independent Meeting House Society was formed and by 1866, it had constructed the Church of the Messiah on the corner of Main and School Streets. The architect of the church was Thomas Silloway, architect of the third and present State House. It is the oldest church structure still standing in Montpelier. (See also photograph in color section.)

The Baptist church organized in Montpelier in 1865 with fourteen members. The church on the corner of St. Paul and School Streets, a wooden structure with many intricate Gothic details, was designed at no cost by architect A.M. Burnham; the construction cost of $17,000 was partially paid for by Jacob Estey of Brattleboro. The first service was held here in the basement in 1868; the church was dedicated in 1873.

Four hundred acres of land were purchased by the village of Montpelier in 1854 for a cemetery. In 1855, Green Mount Cemetery was dedicated in the presence of the Montpelier clergy. (See additional photograph in color section.) "Little Margaret," a granite memorial to six-year-old Margaret Pitkin, is remarkably detailed, down to a missing button on her shoe. It was carved by Harry J. Bertoli of Montpelier, whose granite shed is pictured in Chapter 3.

Chapter 6

Events and Entertainment

Nineteenth- and early twentieth-century Montpelier citizens were no different than residents of other Vermont towns when it came to finding ways to amuse themselves. They played baseball, football and croquet; formed clubs like the Apollo Club; performed in and attended dramatic productions at the Blanchard Opera House; enjoyed state fairs and circuses; visited local watering holes; and went to parades. As the state capital, however, Montpelier has had more events to celebrate than a typical Vermont town of its size: visits from sitting U.S. presidents, state conventions of organizations such as the American Legion and the anniversaries of its own selection as the state capital.

Like many larger Vermont towns, Montpelier had an opera house. Montpelier's was the Blanchard Opera House, a large brick structure on Main Street designed by local architect and future mayor George Guernsey. Opening in 1885, this popular Main Street venue replaced State Street's Capital Hall as the entertainment landmark in town. Its popularity would fade in only twenty-five years, however, as live shows gave way to motion pictures. In 1916, the Play House was built on State Street specifically for the showing of silent movies. When this structure was destroyed by fire in 1939, it was quickly replaced by the Capitol Theater, despite the economic challenges of the Great Depression. The Play House and Capitol Theater weren't even the only theaters in town; numerous early movie theaters dotted Montpelier's downtown, the Savoy and the Strand the most prominent of them.

Since 1895, Montpelier has been home to a notable art collection housed in the T.W. Wood Art Gallery. Montpelier was chosen as the site for this gallery, not because of its prominence as the state capital, but because the nationally recognized artist and gallery donor Thomas Waterman Wood had been born here.

In the winter, Montpelier residents capitalized on the snow for sledding and skating. The Winooski River was a popular site for skating and the hills surrounding downtown were perfect for long sled rides. An especially popular sledding route was down the State Street Extension (later East State Street). Many used a long sled called a traverse. The momentum was said to carry the sledders almost all the way to the State House. This activity was enough of a spectacle that bystanders would line the streets to watch the excitement.

Circuses would visit occasionally in the summer, prompting throngs of people to watch the performers (elephants included) march through the downtown streets. Non-circus parades also drew huge crowds, usually on State and Main Streets. However,

Montpelier's position as state capital also attracted some infamous notoriety. In 1927, the Ku Klux Klan rallied in Montpelier and assembled on Town Hill for a panoramic photograph.

No parade is as well-known in the annals of Montpelier's entertainment past as Dewey Day. Montpelier-born, Spanish-American war hero Admiral George Dewey was thrown an enormous party that thrilled not only the locals but also the thousands who arrived by special trains for the event on October 12, 1899. Dewey's national fame had been achieved one year prior to Dewey Day when, commanding six ships in Manila Bay, his fleet was able to sink every ship in the Spanish fleet. This lopsided defeat opened the door for the American occupation of Manila, and it established the United States as a major naval power. The extravaganza of Dewey Day has never faded from the minds of Montpelierites. In fact, the 100th anniversary of the original Dewey Day was celebrated locally in 1999. Again, bunting adorned many of the downtown buildings that had been draped in similar fashion one hundred years prior.

Another historic celebration that elicited more layers of bunting was the 100th anniversary of Montpelier's being selected as the capital of Vermont, celebrated in 1905. Sorting through images of both the 1899 Dewey Day and the 1905 capital anniversary, it's difficult to distinguish between the two events. Both were attended by massive crowds, had similar decorations and featured activities that extended into the evening.

Montpelier has had several sites for outdoor recreation. First was Langdon Meadow, the wide, flat flood plain of the Winooski River on the western side of town, now the location of the high school. Later, in the 1930s, recreational fields were built along Elm Street. Montpelier has also been fortunate to have a large natural park within its boundaries. In 1899, John E. Hubbard gave the city 125 acres of land behind the State House for a park. In 1911, Jesse S. Viles, former owner of the Pavilion Hotel, deeded additional land to the city, including the highest point behind the State House. Between 1915 and 1931, a picturesque fifty-foot observation tower was built there by contractor John Miglierini from stones found on the property, giving the city one of its most noticeable landmarks.

Although the 1937 WPA guide to Vermont opined about Montpelier, "While the town displays an interest in the cultural phases of life, it remains backward in several respects," the city has shown a significant interest in cultural and recreational pursuits over the course of its 220-year history.

This old engraving is a depiction of one of Vermont's first state fairs, held in Montpelier's Seminary Hill area in 1853. According to a monthly farmers' journal of the time, roughly fifteen to twenty thousand people enjoyed the three-day September event, even with the crowd diminished on the final day due to rain. The grandstand in the center of the illustration held as many as three thousand onlookers. Besides a "trotting course," there were also livestock contests, and local notable Daniel Baldwin won a few awards for his fine livestock. Montpelier would host the event again four years later on the same grounds.

Over the years, circuses have performed in various locations in town, including Langdon Meadow (where the high school is now) and Haymarket Square (where city hall is today). In this early stereoscopic view, a circus is set up on Barre Street where granite sheds would be later built.

The Adam Forepaugh Circus parades up Main Street on July 27, 1883. Montpelier was elated when this circus company chose it as one of the seven cities for a seven-city Vermont tour for the final week of July that year. Most of the local residents and many people from surrounding towns attended the event. Adam Forepaugh proudly boasted that his was the only circus that required three trains to transport. He said that all other circuses at the time only needed one.

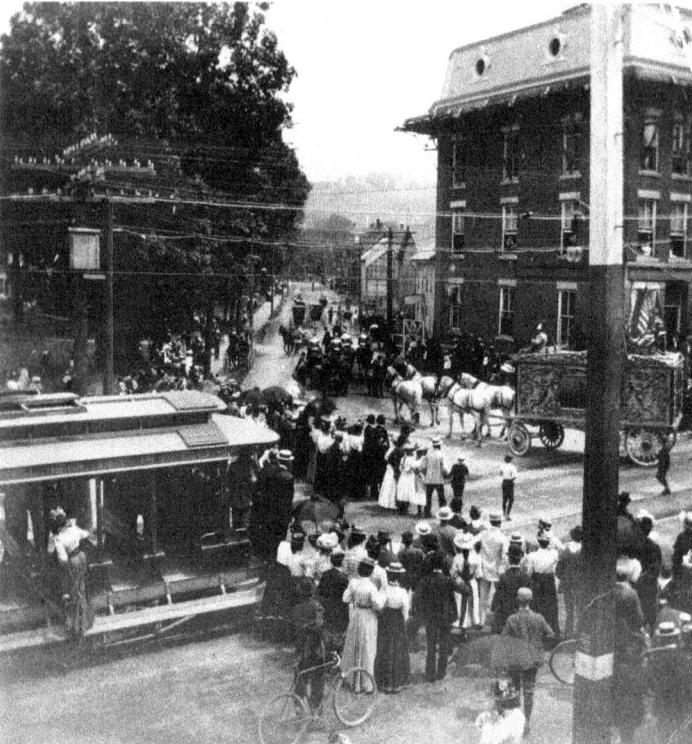

Another parade, this one in 1903, attracted a throng of viewers along its route. This photo was taken at the corner of State and Elm Streets. The trolley (at left) remained stationary for the event, waiting for the end of the circus line to pass.

The ornately detailed library of the Apollo Club, an elite local organization formed in 1884. The group first met in the vestry of the Unitarian church, and moved several times before settling into the Blanchard Block.

The Apollo Club's Blanchard Block pool room in 1893.

The Blanchard Opera House opened in 1885, occupying the second floor of Main Street's Blanchard Block. For a time, the house held three shows per week, and when the trolley began service in 1898, there was even a special "after-show" car that transported audience members home.

The house had about eight hundred seats and, though not seemingly evident in this photo, could also accommodate two hundred standing guests. Unfortunately, the introduction of moving pictures in Montpelier led to waning interest in live events, and the once popular venue staged its final performance on April 1, 1910.

Actors Clarence Pitkin and Edith Adams posed for this promotional photo taken in 1885, the Blanchard Opera House's inaugural year. According to old accounts, Boris Karloff and Eugene O'Neill were among the early stars who performed there, although certainly before they were the household names they would become later. Besides actors, the stage also featured occasional circus events, and there are old accounts of animals (including elephants) being led up the stairs to perform.

The Playhouse, built in 1916, would quickly become Montpelier's first large movie venue. According to advertisements of that era, the first motion picture in color was shown here in 1923, four years before this photo was taken. Unfortunately, this popular theater burned down in 1939.

The interior of the Playhouse as captured in 1928. Until this large theater was built, silent films were shown in various scattered locations downtown. Advertisements for those other venues virtually disappeared in 1916, as the Playhouse became the main location for silent films. Seven years after its grand opening, on March 4, 1923, the first "talkie" was shown here.

After its predecessor (the Playhouse) burned down in 1939, the Capitol Theater was built in the exact same location on State Street. This photo was taken shortly after it opened, as confirmed by 1939's *The Old Maid* on the marquee. Tuttle's (previously Tuttle's Cut Rate Store) shared the building with the Capitol Theater for over twenty years, finally closing in the early 1950s. Originally, the Tuttles owned a store called Ye Old Candy Shoppe, which was next to the Playhouse theater.

The interior of the Capitol Theater took the restrained Art Deco styling of the exterior to a higher level. Because this style was popular during the Depression when few buildings were constructed in Vermont, there are not many examples of it in the state.

The Young Men's Christian Association (YMCA) building was located at 94 State Street, across from the Playhouse and next to the Montpelier House. It was demolished to make way for the expansion of the Tavern Hotel in the 1960s.

Thomas Waterman Wood, a Montpelier native, became an internationally known artist in the second half of the nineteenth century. Many of his figure paintings included Montpelier scenes and people. In August 1895, amidst controversy about the building of the Kellogg-Hubbard Library, Wood gave his paintings to the Wood Art Gallery. The gallery was affiliated with the Montpelier Public Library Association; both were located in the YMCA building, as seen in this 1898 photo. In 1953, the gallery moved into the Kellogg-Hubbard Library, and in 1985 it moved again to Vermont College.

According to an intriguing old caption on the back of this 1890 photo, these bar-goers stand just outside of a saloon (the Soldier's Home) on the corner of School and Elm Streets. The caption identifies the man at the far left as Fred Labershine, and claims he was "pushed off the Union House bridge in 1891 and died in a drunken row."

Langdon Meadow was located beyond the mills and shacks at the western end of Winooski Street along the dirt road to Montpelier Junction. This was the site of circuses, temporary railroad sidings for Dewey Day and ball fields. A temporary footbridge across the Winooski River from State Street to Langdon Meadow was built by civic groups in the early twentieth century to provide access to the recreation area. In 1956, the high school was built on this property, also known at that time as National Life Field.

A total of 3,200 spectators swarmed to the new recreation fields on June 16, 1940, to watch the first baseball game played there. Governor George D. Aiken dedicated the field and then threw out the first ball.

Montpelier High's 1913 championship football team strikes a somewhat unorthodox pose (with either defensive specialists or second stringers standing upright in the back row). In the typical football fashion of that era, no padding is visible, and the linemen appear to be significantly more svelte than they would be on today's teams. Most likely, that's the coach in suit and tie with his hands in his pockets standing on the right.

An action photo of a summertime croquet match at Denison Dewey's house on College Street.

Sledding down East State Street (once known as the State Street extension) was a very popular winter sport in the late 1800s and into the early 1900s. The proliferation of automobiles would finally curb this activity altogether.

Naturally, the best way to accommodate a large group of sledders was to use what was called a "traverse." Here, ten riders pose on their fifteen-foot device in front of the Pavilion Hotel. The traverse was so heavy that a horse would have to haul it to the top of East State Street.

A parade celebrating Decoration Day, which later became known as Memorial Day, marches down Main Street in the 1890s. The building at the left was the armory, also known as the Golden Fleece. The nickname of this structure originated from the presence of a life-sized statue of a ram just outside its front door until the mid-1930s. Unfortunately, no photograph of the ram has been located. (See color section for an additional photograph of the Golden Fleece.)

Special trains brought visitors to Montpelier on October 12, 1899, to celebrate the victory of native son George Dewey over the Spanish fleet in the Battle of Manila Bay a year earlier.

One of the largest events ever hosted in Montpelier, forty thousand visitors flooded into Montpelier for Dewey Day. The entire city was smothered in bunting as Admiral Dewey was carried through the city in a carriage followed by legions of bands and military units.

A typical bunting display for the Dewey Day hoopla was on Main Street's Lawrence block. Not only were photos and prints of Dewey's likeness prominently featured, but a print showing his ship *Olympia* was even posted on many downtown buildings.

The State House wasn't only decked out for the Dewey Day festivities during the day…

…it was also dressed up for that night as well. This electrical undertaking was probably no small feat in 1899.

Left: One feature of the Dewey Day celebration was this immense pyre assembled on the top of the hill behind the State House. The bonfire pile was forty feet in diameter at the base and sixty-nine feet high. It was composed of one thousand barrels, seven hundred railroad ties and the lumber of two buildings. The dogs were present to keep the pile from being ignited prematurely.

Below: The Ellis Block on the north side of State Street was decorated for the parade, and an entrepreneur rented seats to visitors. A man, probably R. Wilkinson, whose studio was in this building, stands on the steps selling stereoviews.

George Dewey's house joined in the gala as well. A souvenir stand was in front and fifteen cents were charged for admission. This house, a notable fixture on the southern side of State Street, had been moved from its original location opposite the State House by Edward Dewey in 1889, and was razed in 1967.

President Theodore Roosevelt came to Montpelier in 1902. His carriage is seen here near the Pavilion Hotel on State Street.

Montpelier matched its enthusiasm for George Dewey with an equal amount of bunting during the 1905 centennial celebration of its being designated the state capital. This is French Block across from city hall on Main Street.

In 1910, the Munsey auto tour came to Montpelier. The tour, which began in Philadelphia, covered 1,530 miles, mostly through the New England states. A total of 115 cars completed the tour, which ended in Washington, D.C., on August 27.

The Munsey parade underway in front of the Pavilion Hotel. Though gaining in popularity, there were still few enough cars in town in 1910 that a gathering of them was a crowd-pleasing spectacle.

In 1912, Montpelier celebrated the 420th anniversary of Columbus's voyage to America with a large parade that lined up along Berlin Street. The Main Street bridge can be seen in the background of the photograph.

The Montpelier Women's Club's float in the Columbus Day parade touted the community's "most valuable natural resource," its children. The Catholic church can be seen in the background of this photograph.

On May 7, 1919, Montpelier's soldiers were welcomed home from World War I in grand fashion. Again, the parade lined up along Berlin Street before heading across the bridge onto Main Street.

The Mount Sinai Temple parade on October 30, 1926, celebrated the Masonic organization's fiftieth anniversary. Crowds lined the streets along State Street and Main Street to watch the parade, which included units from around New England.

On July 4, 1927, members of the Ku Klux Klan paraded through Montpelier in the rain and assembled in a field off Town Hill Road. This is a portion of a larger panoramic photograph. The event was the only KKK rally known to have taken place in the city.

Two years later, the American Legion sponsored a parade that filled the streets with onlookers who watched a band maneuver around the traffic control device in the middle of the intersection of State and Main Streets.

Elephants were part of this firemen's convention parade in 1935, selected perhaps because of their ability to spray water. The large animals became the perfect vehicle for advertising; the lead elephant here was equipped with a sign advertising Studebaker automobiles.

Montpelier's drum and bugle corps participated in the Preparedness Day parade on Main Street in September 1940, more than a year before the United States entered World War II. The high school students in the foreground joined the parade and marched a mile to the new recreation field on Elm Street for a football game against Barre's Spaulding High School. Across the street were Gray's Department Store and other stores now long gone from the downtown scene.

Chapter 7

Fires and Floods

Montpelier has had its share of natural and man-made disasters. In terms of property loss, the most devastating disasters to leave scars on Montpelier were the two downtown fires of 1875 and the flood of 1927, but numerous smaller and less traumatic fires and floods have beset Montpelier over the years as well.

The 1875 fires were a serious wake-up call to a city that had been through many small-scale blazes over the years. The night of March 12 was particularly windy when the first fire erupted. No one knows exactly what caused the fire, but the flames originated in a carpenter's shop owned by Thomas Waterman Wood that sat just behind a building on the west side of Main Street. The flames emanating from the shop spread quickly to the south side of State Street and then managed to cross to the east side of Main. Nine buildings were completely destroyed, despite valiant efforts to save them.

As the city was starting to rebuild, a second fire erupted at the dawn of May. This one began about a half hour earlier than its predecessor and originated not far from the earlier one. This second fire was also fueled by a strong breeze, and consumed most of the buildings on the west side of Main Street. In desperation, people who considered their belongings in jeopardy frantically heaved their belongings into the middle of Main Street. Unfortunately, the fire found these items all too easily as it crossed the street. It was reported that the towering flames could be seen from towns ten miles away. In all, thirty-eight buildings were destroyed and yet there were no deaths reported as a result of either fire.

Though seriously beaten by two major fires within two months of one another, Montpelier again demonstrated its steadfast resilience. Architectural designs and plans for redevelopment were drawn up within several weeks of the second fire. This time, however, the town adopted a crucial architectural safeguard: there would be no more large wooden structures built downtown. Of the thirty-eight buildings annihilated in the second fire, thirty-five had been of wood construction. It has been claimed that in the aftermath of the May fire, the town even went so far as to cite a local builder for beginning to construct a downtown barn.

Fifty-two years later, another disaster brought about a new set of structural changes to downtown Montpelier. The city had been prone to flooding, but the severity of the flood of early November 1927 was a surprise to residents. Rivers were swollen and the ground was saturated when a tropical storm dumped seven to nine inches of rain on the state over a period of three days. In Montpelier, the waters crested at twelve feet above street level on the morning of November 4. Eighty-five Vermonters died, including one in Montpelier, and nine thousand were left homeless statewide. Property losses in Montpelier averaged $400 for every resident. As witness to just how tumultuous this event was locally, there are still high-water marks indelibly etched on plaques in many of the city's downtown buildings.

The 1927 deluge necessitated the rebuilding of bridges in Montpelier. Of the twenty-four bridges in the city, only seven remained undamaged. The Taylor Street, Pioneer Street, School Street and Langdon Street bridges, along with eight smaller bridges, all had to be replaced. About eighteen thousand books had to be discarded from the Kellogg-Hubbard Library and some buildings, such as Bethany Church and the Baptist church, never fully recovered from the damage they suffered during the flood.

Around New England, flood control dams were built to prevent a recurrence of the tragic event. A dam was built on the North Branch of the Winooski River, intentionally obliterating the community known as Wrightsville. Straddling the Montpelier/Middlesex town line, the community had a proud history as a lumbering and manufacturing village. The dam was constructed by members of the Civilian Conservation Corps and was dedicated by President Franklin D. Roosevelt in 1936.

The disasters of the past have in many ways affected the appearance of present-day Montpelier. The city's downtown brick buildings and steel truss bridges are both the result of disasters that struck the city. Other individual buildings had to be replaced or rebuilt because of fires or floods. Despite these setbacks, or perhaps because of them, Montpelier has emerged with a strong architectural and historical identity.

The 1869 flood devastated Montpelier more than any other flood that had come before it. Possibly to demonstrate how deep it is, a man wades through the floodwaters on State Street.

Another of Montpelier's many floods, this one occurring in 1887. This image shows the south bank of the Winooski River looking east, as seen from the Arch Bridge at Main Street.

From the hill on the south side of the Winooski River, overlooking Main Street and the North Branch (in the center of this image), this photo shows how much property was consumed by the 1875 fires.

The second 1875 fire managed to cross Main Street and ravage many structures on Barre Street. A great many of the fire aftermath photos were taken by Charles H. Freeman, a significant fact in that Freeman lost his own State Street studio in the second fire. Freeman, whose photos are featured prominently throughout this work, would leave Montpelier not long after his studio burned.

Onlookers assess the damage to buildings on State Street after the second 1875 fire. The steeple of the Episcopal church is in the distance.

Taken just a few weeks after the second fire, this State Street photo clearly depicts a rebuilding effort already beginning. Notice the sawhorse and other construction materials on the Rialto Bridge. The corner of Main and Barre Streets is at the upper right of the photograph.

Demonstrating adaptation to this major inconvenience, intrepid rowboaters ride out the 1900 flood on Main Street north of State Street. The Unitarian church is in the distance.

Another view of the 1900 flood, showing the Union House at the corner of School and Main Streets and the billiard hall behind it.

A fire breaks out on the west side of Main Street in 1906, drawing a crowd. These flames originated in the back of the Massucco Block, the three-story building right of center in the photograph.

The day after a February 15, 1914 fire on State Street, icicles from the water used to quell the flames create a visually interesting effect for visitors. The tower of city hall on Main Street peeks out from behind the destruction.

The bridge over the North Branch appears to have been a very useful platform from which to fight this 1911 fire. Unfortunately, this building would topple and fall into the river soon after this action photo was snapped.

The heroic efforts to help potential victims of the 1911 fire were performed by the volunteer fire department. The advent of a select few paid firefighters was still more than a decade away.

The old E.W. Bailey Grist Mill, a fixture on Main Street across from Barre Street for many years, crumples as the result of a fire in 1923. It was replaced by a modern concrete grain elevator that would stand in the same location until the early 1960s. The Colton shops on the other side of the Winooski River are in the background.

A tragic Main Street fire in 1924 not only devastated the Lawrence Block, but also took eleven lives, the most of any fire in Montpelier's history. An even more tragic footnote, two of the deaths occurred as a result of jumpers simply missing the safety net stretched out by firefighters below.

Taken from the Rialto Block early on the morning of November 4, 1927, this view of State Street illustrates the magnitude of the 1927 flood. Many of the buildings on both State and Main Streets still have plaques showing their high-water mark for this catastrophe.

This photo, taken on November 5, 1927, was shot from the Rialto Bridge, facing the North Branch. Underneath this debris are the abutments of the Langdon Street Bridge. That bridge was washed away, one of twelve local bridges that couldn't withstand the rising floodwaters. The wreckage shown here was very typical of the damage done by the flood all over the state.

Visit us at
www.historypress.net

www.ingramcontent.com/pod-product-compliance
Lightning Source LLC
Chambersburg PA
CBHW080920100426
42812CB00007B/2328